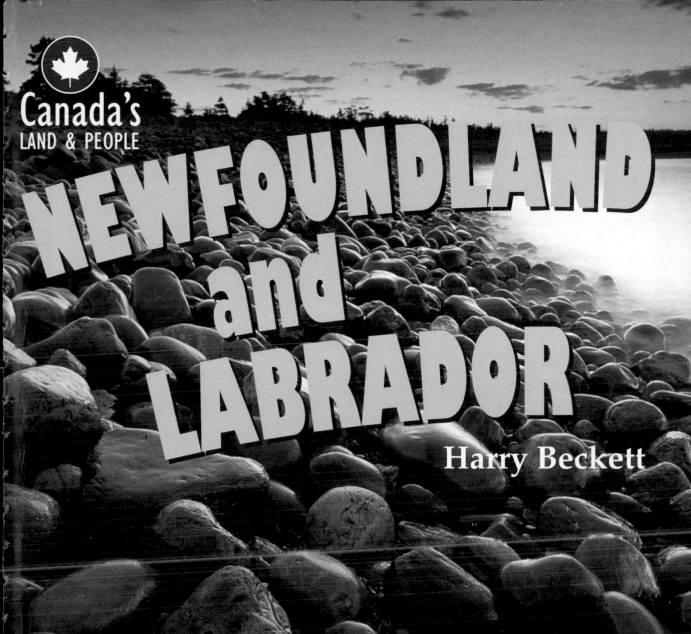

Canada's
LAND & PEOPLE

NEWFOUNDLAND
and
LABRADOR

Harry Beckett

Weigl
CALGARY
www.weigl.com

Published by Weigl Educational Publishers Limited
6325 10 Street SE
Calgary, Alberta   T2H 2Z9

Website: www.weigl.com
Copyright ©2008 Weigl Educational Publishers Limited

Library and Archives Canada Cataloguing in Publication

Beckett, Harry, 1936-
    Newfoundland and Labrador / Harry Beckett.

(Canada's land and people)
Includes index.
ISBN 978-1-55388-361-6 (bound)
ISBN 978-1-55388-362-3 (pbk.)

    1. Newfoundland and Labrador--Juvenile literature. I. Title.
II. Series.
FC2161.2.B435 2007   j971.8   C2007-902204-9

Printed in the United States of America
1 2 3 4 5 6 7 8 9 0 11 10 09 08 07

We acknowledge the financial support of the Government of Canada through the Book Publishing Industry Development Program (BPIDP) for our publishing activities.

Photograph credits: Roy D. McLaren: page 9 middle left; Memorial University of Newfoundland: page 15 middle left; Ned Pratt (courtesy of The Rooms Corporation of Newfoundland and Labrador): page 15 bottom; Saint John's Folk Art Council: page 15 middle right.

Project Coordinator
Heather C. Hudak

Design
Terry Paulhus

Contents

About Newfoundland and Labrador

Newfoundland is an island in the Atlantic Ocean. Labrador is part of Canada's mainland, just north of Newfoundland. Together, they cover 405,720 square kilometres of land. They form Canada's seventh largest and most eastern province.

Newfoundland and Labrador joined Confederation on March 31, 1949. The province is Canada's tenth and newest province.

In 1497, Italian explorer John Cabot sighted a "new found isle." The British called the area "new founde launde" in the 1500s. Canada officially changed the name from Newfoundland to Newfoundland and Labrador on December 6, 2001.

In 1827, Great Britain approved the official mace for Newfoundland and Labrador. The crown at the top honours the province's ties to Great Britain. The three dolphins show the importance of the sea and fishing.

ABOUT THE FLAG

Newfoundland and Labrador's flag became official on June 6, 1980. The white field stands for snow and ice. Blue shows the sea. Red celebrates hard work. The golden arrow points to a bright future. The two outlined triangles represent the mainland and the island coming together.

LEGEND

N

Yukon

Northwest Territories

Nunavut

British Columbia

Alberta

Manitoba

Saskatchewan

Ontario

Quebec

Newfoundland and Labrador

Prince Edward Island

New Brunswick

Nova Scotia

ACTION Make a small mace for the place where you live. Use a tube from a roll of paper towel. Decorate the tube with colours and shapes that show what is important to you and your neighbours.

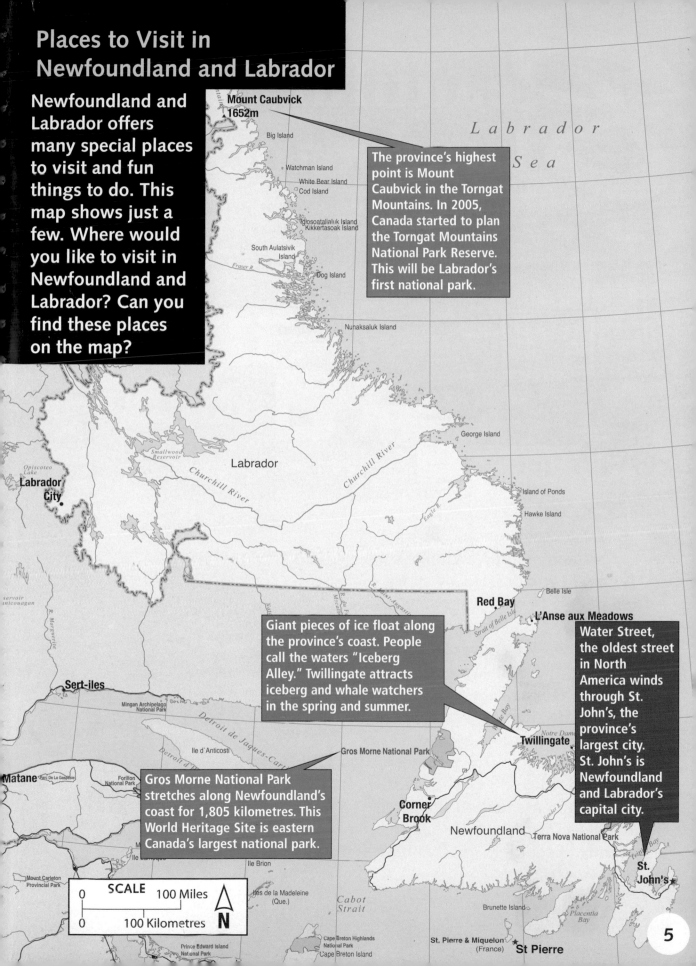

Places to Visit in Newfoundland and Labrador

Newfoundland and Labrador offers many special places to visit and fun things to do. This map shows just a few. Where would you like to visit in Newfoundland and Labrador? Can you find these places on the map?

The province's highest point is Mount Caubvick in the Torngat Mountains. In 2005, Canada started to plan the Torngat Mountains National Park Reserve. This will be Labrador's first national park.

Giant pieces of ice float along the province's coast. People call the waters "Iceberg Alley." Twillingate attracts iceberg and whale watchers in the spring and summer.

Water Street, the oldest street in North America winds through St. John's, the province's largest city. St. John's is Newfoundland and Labrador's capital city.

Gros Morne National Park stretches along Newfoundland's coast for 1,805 kilometres. This World Heritage Site is eastern Canada's largest national park.

Map labels:

Mount Caubvick 1652m
Big Island
Watchman Island
White Bear Island
Cod Island
Igloosoatalialuk Island
Kikkertasoak Island
South Aulatsivik Island
Fraser R.
Dog Island
Nunaksaluk Island

Labrador Sea

Labrador
Smallwood Reservoir
Churchill River
Churchill River
George Island
Opiscoteo Lake
Labrador City
Island of Ponds
Hawke Island
Eagle R.

servoir nicouagan
R. Marguerile
Belle Isle
Red Bay
L'Anse aux Meadows
Strait of Belle Isle

Sert-iles
Mingan Archipelago National Park
Detroit de Jacques-Cart...
Detroit d'...
Ile d'Anticosti

Matane
Bais De La Gaspésie
Forillon National Park
Gros Morne National Park
Twillingate
Notre Dam...
Corner Brook
Gander R.
Newfoundland
Terra Nova National Park

Mount Carleton Provincial Park
Ile Lameque
Ile Brion
St. John's

SCALE
0 — 100 Miles
0 — 100 Kilometres
N

Iles de la Madeleine (Que.)
Cabot Strait
Brunette Island
Placentia Bay
Prince Edward Island National Park
Cape Breton Highlands National Park
Cape Breton Island
St. Pierre & Miquelon (France)
St Pierre

Beautiful Landscapes

Rocky coasts border the rugged wilderness of Newfoundland and Labrador. Heavy snow, often deeper than 300 centimetres, covers most of the province each winter. When the snow melts in the spring, the fresh water fills the province's many rivers and lakes. Summers are short and cool, with average temperatures around 13 degrees Celsius. Warm weather from the deep south clashes with cold sea currents just off the coast and makes fog. Fog drifts over the eastern and southern coasts about 124 days each year.

Ancient, hard rock from the Canadian Shield covers most of Labrador. Polar bears, musk-ox, and other cold-weather animals live in northern Labrador's windy **tundra**.

The Long Range Mountains overlook Newfoundland's western shore. They are part of the **Appalachian range** that reaches into the southern United States.

The boreal forest covers about 30 percent of the province. Aspen, birch, balsam fir, and white and black spruce trees live in the boreal forest. The province's forest industry harvests trees mainly for newsprint.

The Atlantic Uplands includes eastern areas of Newfoundland. Between the rolling hills are bogs, ponds, and small lakes.

The province is nicknamed "The Rock" for its rough and rocky landscape. Jagged cliffs stand above saltwater bays in many parts of Newfoundland.

Fur, Feathers, and Flowers

The province of Newfoundland and Labrador has fewer animals and plants than other provinces because of its harsh weather and rocky soil. Labrador has about 40 native mammals, such as the barren-ground caribou, mink, wolverine, and arctic wolf. Only 14 of those mammals live on the island of Newfoundland. Many plants and animals, such as the moose and red squirrel, came to the island with European settlers in the 1600s.

Newfoundland and Labrador's official bird is the Atlantic Puffin. Nearly all of North America's puffins live along the province's coasts.

The province's official tree is the black spruce. The tree looks bluish-green, not black. Labrador has more black spruce than any other kind of tree.

The Labrador husky and Newfoundland pony are important to the province's history. The 1996 Heritage Animals Act protects these winter-hardy animals, because their breeds are disappearing. Today, fewer than 200 Newfoundland ponies exist.

The province's official game bird is the partridge or ptarmigan. It lives in wilderness areas across the region.

The pitcher plant catches water in its leaves. Insects drown in the small pools, and the plant eats them. During colonial times, Aboriginal Peoples treated **smallpox** with this wetland plant. The pitcher plant became the province's official flower in 1954.

Rich in Resources

Fishing first attracted Europeans to Newfoundland and Labrador in the 1500s. By the 1900s, pulp and paper manufacturing and **iron ore** mining became important industries. In the 1990s, oil and natural gas deposits brought jobs to the province. Today, the province's main products include fish and seafood, newsprint, and refined **petroleum**, such as gasoline. Tourism helps the province's economy, too.

The Grand Banks fishery is located off Newfoundland's southeastern coast. It ranks among the world's best. Strict laws help guard against too much fishing. Instead of wild catches, fish farms produce steady supplies of salmon, trout, and mussels.

Blueberries and other wild berries grow well in Labrador. They are some of the few crops exported by Newfoundland and Labrador.

The province is Canada's leading producer of iron ore for making steel. Newfoundland and Labrador also has deposits of silver, gold, limestone, gypsum, nickel, and other minerals.

The Hibernia oil-drilling rig started working in 1997 off the Grand Banks. It is the world's largest drilling platform. It drills oil out of the ocean bed. Designers built the Hibernia rig to withstand an unlikely crash with a 6-million-tonne iceberg.

Shaped by History

Only the Beothuk Aboriginal Peoples lived on Newfoundland in the 1500s when Europeans arrived. European diseases and a First Nations war killed many of the Beothuks. The last known Beothuk died in 1829. Other Aboriginal Peoples lived in present-day Labrador. The Inuit lived mainly in central Labrador and along the mainland coast. The Innu lived to the north of the Inuit. Both groups moved from camp to camp to hunt and gather food. Today, Aboriginal communities can be found throughout the province. The Inuit and First Nation peoples, such as the Mi'kmaq, celebrate their traditions with songs, dances, food, and storytelling.

The first Europeans to explore North America were likely Norse sailors. Scientists believe they landed near present-day L'Anse aux Meadows in Newfoundland in AD 986. Today, a national park at the site features actors in costumes to help explain how these earliest settlers lived.

About 500 years after Norse sailors arrived, John Cabot sailed from Great Britain to Newfoundland. He reported seas thick with fish. Spain, France, and Great Britain sent fishing fleets in the 1500s. Settlers arrived in the early 1600s. Most came from Great Britain.

Great Britain and France battled to own the region in the 1700s. Great Britain won but gave France fishing rights. The French received the islands of Saint-Pierre et Miquelon, just off Newfoundland's southern shore.

In 1809, Newfoundland claimed Labrador from Quebec. The additional mainland gave Newfoundland more area for fishing, seal hunting, and fur trading. Many Irish people came to Newfoundland and Labrador looking for work along the Labrador coast. Harbours grew into busy communities. The Irish culture is still strong in the province today.

Art and Culture

People from other places found it difficult to travel to Newfoundland and Labrador until modern airplane service started in the region. With few people from other places, the province's arts and culture stayed connected to many European traditions. Fiddle and accordion music, storytelling, and dancing are common folk arts. Today, the province's people still speak with words and phrases not used in other places. A small tin cup is a "bannikin." A tourist is called a "come-from-away." Messy hair is "all mops and brooms."

Mummers follow an old British Christmas tradition. They wear silly costumes and paint their faces. Some perform plays or dance in the streets. Mummers might visit neighbours' houses. The hosts try to guess who the mummers are.

For more than 40 years, the Newfoundland and Labrador Folk Festival has celebrated the province's heritage through music, dance, and crafts. Thousands of people gather at Bannerman Park in St. John's each summer for the event.

Memorial University of Newfoundland is the province's only university and the largest in Canada's Atlantic region. Its main campus is in St. John's.

The Rooms in St. John's keeps many historical items. It also has a natural history collection and **relics** of the Beothuk people.

Points of Interest

Newfoundland and Labrador has three national parks. Two of them, L'Anse aux Meadows National Park and Gros Morne National Park, have been named World Heritage Sites because of their importance to all humans. Terra Nova National Park in eastern Newfoundland became the province's first national park in 1957. Newfoundland and Labrador supports 70 provincial parks and other special areas set aside to protect wildlife.

Guglielmo Marconi invented the radio. He received the first **transatlantic** wireless message at Signal Hill in 1901. Cabot Tower was built in 1897 at Signal Hill to honour the 400th anniversary of John Cabot's voyage to the region. The tower also celebrated Queen Victoria's 60th anniversary as Great Britain's queen. Today, Signal Hill is a national historic park.

Cape Spear is North America's most easterly point. Canada's oldest standing lighthouse is there.

Many bird **sanctuaries** across Newfoundland and Labrador protect nesting grounds for seabirds and migrating birds. Birdwatchers come from all over the world to Cape St. Mary's. It has one of the world's largest seabird **rookeries**.

During the 1500s, French and Spanish whale hunters gathered in the safe harbour of Red Bay along the Labrador coast. Summer visitors can explore this part of the province's past at the Red Bay National Historic Site of Canada.

Sports and Activities

Newfoundland and Labrador's untamed landscape attracts outdoor adventurers. They camp, fish, hike, bike, snowshoe, ski, and snowmobile in wilderness areas across the province. Newfoundland and Labrador does not have any major-league sports teams. Hockey, basketball, and other team sports bring **amateur** players together at local schools and recreation centres.

The St. John's Fog Devils play in the Quebec Hockey League. This Junior "A" team helps train young players for professional hockey.

Since 1818, the Royal St. John's Regatta has brought rowing athletes and fans to the city. The event is now an official city holiday.

The Newfoundland Trailway, now a provincial park, follows an old rail line across the island of Newfoundland. Hikers, mountain-bike riders, and snowmobilers enjoy the trail.

Every year in March, **mushers** from around the world meet in Labrador City for the Labrador 400 dogsled race. The dog teams cover 644 kilometres as they charge to Churchill Falls and back.

What Others Are Saying

Many people have great things to say about Newfoundland and Labrador.

"Of all the cities I have written about, anywhere in the world, none has given me more enjoyment than St. John's, Newfoundland, the most entertaining town in North America."

"With its own dialect, frequent insulating fogs, its own diverse traditions, and even its own time zone, thirty minutes off everyone else's, Newfoundland is connected to the mainland by airplanes that are often crippled by the thick fog, by storm-tossed ferries that must also be icebreakers to dodge icebergs..."

"Come on over here (NL) to see a distinct society. This is like no other place. People say it is like Europe, but it's not, there's something different here; it's about here. This is where it is. This is who it is; it has sprung out of the land."

British Poet Lord Byron honoured his Newfoundland dog with a monument. He wrote about his dog in a poem: "The poor dog, in life the firmest friend; The first to welcome, foremost to defend."

ACTION Think about the place where you live. Come up with some words to describe your province, city, or community. Are there rolling hills and deep valleys? Can you see trees or lakes? What are some of the features of the land, people, and buildings that make your home special? Use these words to write a paragraph about the place where you live.

Test Your Knowledge

What have you learned about Newfoundland and Labrador? Try answering the following questions.

 **1** Where is L'Anse aux Meadows National Park located? What is special about this park?

 2 Which European groups first fished in the waters off Newfoundland and Labrador? What sea animals did they catch?

3 Search for books in the library, or research on the internet to learn more about Newfoundland and Labrador's Grand Banks and the fish that live there. Write a paragraph about the Grand Banks and its habitat. Explain how laws can help protect Canada's fish.

Create an Official Animal

Interesting and unusual animals live in Newfoundland and Labrador. Select one that you would like to become the province's official animal. Use the internet to help you learn more about the animal and its habitat. Draw a picture of it. Write a paragraph about why you chose this animal and what it means to people who live in Newfoundland and Labrador.

Further Research

Books

To find out more about Newfoundland and Labrador and other Canadian provinces and territories, visit your local library. Most libraries have computers that connect to a database for researching information. If you input a key word, you will be provided with a list of books in the library that contain information on that topic. Non-fiction books are arranged numerically, using their call number. Fiction books are organized alphabetically by the author's last name.

Websites

The World Wide Web is a good source of information. Reliable websites usually include government sites, educational sites, and online encyclopedias. Visit the following sites to learn more about Newfoundland and Labrador.

Go to the Government of Newfoundland and Labrador's website to learn about the province's government, history, and climate.
www.gov.nf.ca

Visit the Newfoundland and Labrador Heritage site to learn more about the province's past.
www.heritage.nf.ca

The Innu website offers information about the language, culture, and concerns of this First Nations Group.
www.innu.ca

Glossary

amateur: a person who plays a game for fun, not for money or as a job

Appalachian range: a line of mountains in eastern North America stretching from Quebec to the Gulf of Mexico

iron ore: a grey or red rock that contains iron for making steel

mummers: silent actors who act silly and play a traditional European guessing game

mushers: dogsled drivers

petroleum: liquid oil for fuel

relics: objects from the past made by humans

rookeries: breeding grounds or nesting areas for birds of the same kind

sanctuaries: places that protect wildlife and usually do not allow hunting

smallpox: a very contagious and deadly disease in humans that is now prevented by a vaccine

transatlantic: crossing the Atlantic Ocean

tundra: a treeless, mossy, and windy plain

Index